Fact Finders®

Landmarks in U.S. History

The Perils of the
Santa Fe Trail

by Jean K. Williams

CAPSTONE PRESS
a capstone imprint

Fact Finder Books are published by Capstone Press,
1710 Roe Crest Drive, North Mankato, Minnesota 56003
www.mycapstone.com

Library of Congress Cataloging-in-Publication Data
Names: Williams, Jean Kinney, author.
Title: The perils of the Santa Fe Trail / by Jean K. Williams.
Description: North Mankato, Minnesota : Capstone Press, [2017] | Series: Fact
    finders. Landmarks in U.S. history | Includes bibliographical references
    and index. | Audience: Grades 4–6. | Audience: Ages 8–10.
Identifiers: LCCN 2017003799 (print) | LCCN 2017004631 (ebook) |
    ISBN 9781515771173 (library hardcover) | ISBN 9781515771401 (pbk.) |
    ISBN 9781515771449 (eBook PDF)
Subjects: LCSH: Santa Fe National Historic Trail—Juvenile literature. | West
    (U.S.)—Description and travel—Juvenile literature.
Classification: LCC F786 .W737 2017 (print) | LCC F786 (ebook) | DDC 978—dc23
LC record available at https://lccn.loc.gov/2017003799

Editorial Credits
Bradley Cole and Gena Chester, editors; Sarah Bennett, designer; Pam Mitsakos, media researcher;
Steve Walker, production specialist

Photo Credits
Getty Images: Corbis, 12–13 bottom, Corbis/Library of Congress, 1, Karl Gehring/The Denver Post,
16–17, SuperStock, 23, Universal History Archive/UIG, 26–27; Newscom: akg-images, 10 bottom, Album/
Florilegius, 14–15; North Wind Picture Archives: cover, 4–5, 6–7, 19, 20–21, 24, 28–29; Shutterstock:
Everett Historical, 8 inset, Marco Prati, 11, Sue Smith, 13 top right inset, Zack Frank, 8 background; XNR
Productions: XNR/Map, 9

Design Elements:
Shutterstock: Andrey_Kuzmin, ilolab, Jacob J. Rodriguez-Call, Jessie Eldora Robertson, Olga Rutko

Printed and bound in the USA
010399F17

TABLE OF CONTENTS

OPENING UP THE SOUTHWEST

The sharp crack of a bullwhip and the cries of the drivers echoed through the air. Thousands of heavy **freight** wagons headed out of Missouri bound for Santa Fe, New Mexico. The wagons creaked as the oxen strained to pull them.

The wagons carried goods to sell in Santa Fe. Starting in 1804, **pioneers** using the route opened up the southwestern United States to settlement. The route was called the Santa Fe Trail.

The trail wove through what would become five states — Kansas, Oklahoma, Colorado, Texas, and New Mexico. Forts and trading posts sprang up along the trail. Pioneers traveled the trail and settled in the new states. All of the trips, forts, and trading posts helped America grow.

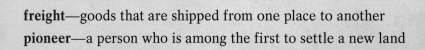

freight—goods that are shipped from one place to another

pioneer—a person who is among the first to settle a new land

4

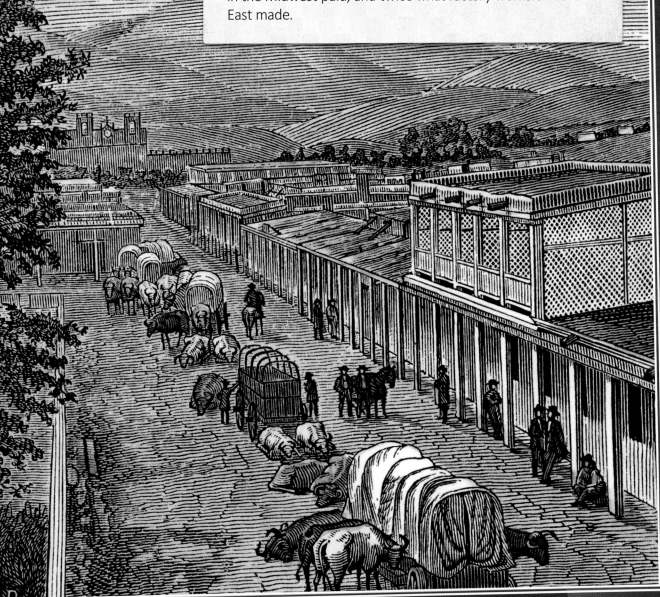

Better Wages

Life on the trail and in the West was dangerous but offered better wages. Men rarely earned more than a dollar a day on the East Coast of the United States. Pay for jobs, such as factory work, varied widely. The size of the factory, what the factory produced, and what positions people worked all affected the workers' pay. Farmhands in California could earn $60 a month. That wage was four times what most places in the Midwest paid, and twice what factory workers in the East made.

Covered wagons reach the end of the Santa Fe Trail in New Mexico.

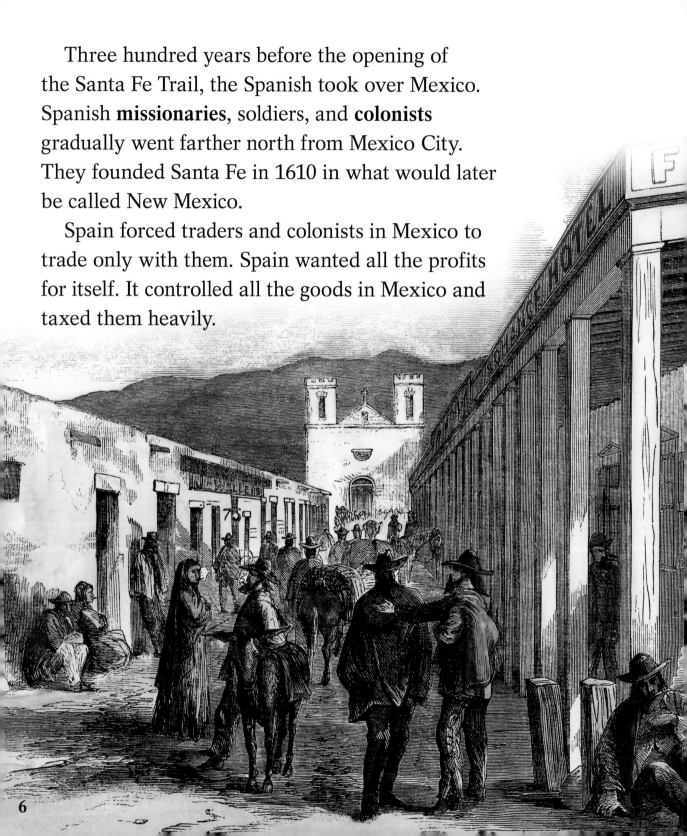

Three hundred years before the opening of
the Santa Fe Trail, the Spanish took over Mexico.
Spanish **missionaries**, soldiers, and **colonists**
gradually went farther north from Mexico City.
They founded Santa Fe in 1610 in what would later
be called New Mexico.

Spain forced traders and colonists in Mexico to
trade only with them. Spain wanted all the profits
for itself. It controlled all the goods in Mexico and
taxed them heavily.

Mexico won its independence from Spain in 1821. The people of Santa Fe were eager to buy North American goods. Traders, such as William Becknell, wanted customers in this new market. Becknell was in Colorodo trading at the time of Mexico's independence. He rushed through the 8,000-foot (2,438-meter) high Raton Pass in the Sangre de Cristo Mountains into New Mexico. This route became known as the Mountain Branch.

After trading in Santa Fe, Becknell went home to Franklin, Missouri. He used his profits to buy huge amounts of luxury items, such as fabrics, mirrors, and jewelry. He also bought three wagons and oxen to carry all the goods. With 21 strong men to help, he again set out for Santa Fe in 1822.

The Plaza, shown here, was the center of trading in Santa Fe.

colonist—a person who settles in a new territory that is governed by his or her home country

missionary—a person who does religious or charitable work in a territory or foreign country

Becknell didn't think his wagons could make it through Raton Pass. Instead, he took what came to be called the Cimarron Cutoff. **Legend** says that the first trip through the Cimarron Cutoff was hard. Becknell and his crew didn't find water for three days. But the challenges paid off when Becknell finally sold his goods.

The next year many followed the Cimarron trail. A **caravan** of 25 wagons set off from Franklin in 1824. They carried $35,000 worth of goods and sold them in Santa Fe at a profit of $155,000.

A young **apprentice** in Franklin eagerly watched the wagons gather and depart for two years. Christopher "Kit" Carson hated his work in the harness shop. He wanted to join the caravan, so he ran away with a **wagon train** in 1824.

Christopher "Kit" Carson

DID YOU KNOW?
As a general rule, people can go three minutes without air, three days without water, and three weeks without food. This is why most of the Santa Fe Trail followed access to water.

Carson became a famous pioneer of the trail. He spent most of his life as a frontiersman, hunter, guide, and army scout. He died on the trail in Fort Lyon, Colorado, after being thrown from a horse in 1868.

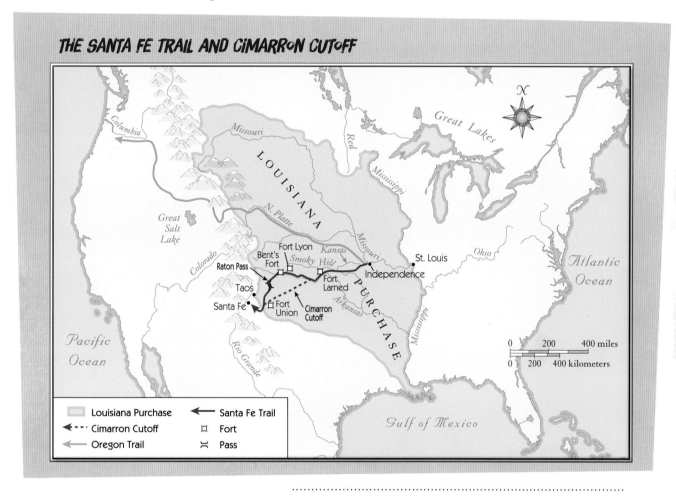

THE SANTA FE TRAIL AND CIMARRON CUTOFF

legend—a story passed down through the years that may not be completely true

caravan—a group of wagons traveling together

apprentice—someone who learns a trade by working with a skilled person

wagon train—a group of pioneers traveling together in covered wagons, often in a single-file line

THE ROUTE OUT OF MISSOURI

In 1821 the trail started in Franklin, Missouri. At the time Franklin was the town farthest west in Missouri. But floods destroyed Franklin in 1826. By that time a new town called Independence, Missouri, was founded. Independence became the new **trailhead** of the Santa Fe Trail. Because Independence was 131 miles (211 kilometers) west of Franklin, the trail to Santa Fe would be shorter from there.

Independence, Missouri, around 1855

DID YOU KNOW?

Buffalo are only found in Africa and Asia. Bison are from North America and can run as fast as 40 miles (64 km) per hour. They can weigh as much as 1,400 pounds (635 kilograms).

After leaving Independence, settlers saw nothing but bison and treeless prairie for days. After 120 miles (193 km), they reached Council Grove, a town on the Neosho River. The change of scenery was welcome. The stop gave the traders a chance to repair their wagons and to rest in the shade. A large oak tree at the site served as a trail post office. People traveling west left letters in the tree. The letters were picked up and delivered for mailing by people traveling east.

trailhead—the point at which a trail begins

THE CUTOFF AND THE MOUNTAIN BRANCH

At first the Santa Fe Trail followed the Kansas River before switching to follow the Arkansas River in western Kansas. The trail continued on to follow the Arkansas River through Kansas. In 1859 the U.S. government set up Fort Larned along the river to help protect travelers. Even though the fort was on American Indian land, tribes did not attack it — just pioneers on the trail. However, the Kiowa tribe once stole 172 horses from Fort Larned.

As the trail and river neared Dodge City, Kansas, pioneers had to choose between the Mountain Branch and the Cimarron Cutoff. The Mountain Branch was about 900 miles (1,448 km) long and stayed safely away from Comanche territory. While using the Cimarron Cutoff increased the risk of American Indian attacks, it also shortened the trail by 100 miles (161 km).

Dangerous River Crossings

River in territories did not have bridges, so pioneers looked for shallow water when crossing. Fording rivers — crossing shallow points — was one of the most dangerous parts of traveling by wagon. Before crossing, pioneers waterproofed the wagons by filling in cracks with a wax paste made from candles and ash. Settlers and animals would swim across, while oxen or mules would pull the wagons through the river. Wagons could tip, and people could drown. Sometimes the river was too high to ford. Pioneers would try and float their wagons across the river — an even more dangerous situation.

Soldiers at Fort Larned protected the Santa Fe Trail 70 miles (113 km) either way from the fort.

The history of Comanche attacks against caravans on the Cimarron Cutoff began in 1828. Two traders named Robert McNees and Daniel Monroe had ridden ahead of their caravan. They were waiting at a creek when a group of American Indians — from which tribe, no one knows — shot at them. When the caravan arrived, McNees was dead, and Monroe was wounded.

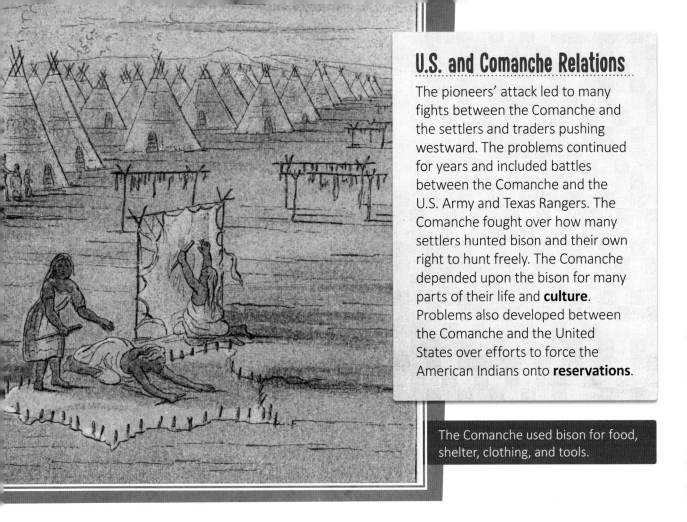

U.S. and Comanche Relations

The pioneers' attack led to many fights between the Comanche and the settlers and traders pushing westward. The problems continued for years and included battles between the Comanche and the U.S. Army and Texas Rangers. The Comanche fought over how many settlers hunted bison and their own right to hunt freely. The Comanche depended upon the bison for many parts of their life and **culture**. Problems also developed between the Comanche and the United States over efforts to force the American Indians onto **reservations**.

The Comanche used bison for food, shelter, clothing, and tools.

The next American Indians the caravan saw were the Comanche. The pioneers did not stop to discover whether the Comanche were the ones who had killed McNees. They shot at the Comanche. The Comanche who escaped warned the others. The tribe struggled against white pioneers along the Cimarron Cutoff for many years.

culture—a people's way of life, ideas, art, customs, and traditions
reservation—an area of land set aside by the U.S. government for American Indians

Many pioneer families were willing to take the longer Mountain Branch route into Santa Fe to avoid the Comanche. These groups continued along the Arkansas River until they reached Bent's Fort. There, the trail turned south through the Sangre de Cristo Mountains.

Charles and William Bent were young trappers. They sold furs and bought goods to take on the Santa Fe Trail in 1829. They had a trading post built along the Mountain Branch. Mexican workers built the square **adobe** structure. It had 25 rooms around an open courtyard. The fort was first known as Fort William and later as Bent's Fort.

William Bent was married to a Cheyenne named Owl Woman. Unlike the Comanche, the Cheyenne were friendly and easy trading partners. The Cheyenne and other American Indian tribes met peaceably at Bent's Fort.

adobe—a brick building material made of clay mixed with straw and dried in the sun

Furs, horses, tobacco, and bison robes were just some of the goods traded at the fort.

During the Mexican-American War (1846–1848), U.S. troops captured New Mexico in 1846. Charles Bent became its governor. He lived in Taos with his wife, Maria Ignacia Jaramillo. Taos rebels — local Mexicans and Taos Indians — murdered Charles the following year. The fort reminded William of the death of his brother. Because of this, he grew to hate the fort. He had everything removed and blew up the huge structure.

Even in ruins, Bent's Fort was an important marker on the way to Raton Pass. The pass was a hair-raising part of the journey. The downward path was so steep that a wagon's wheels had to be locked. The strongest men had to lower the wagons down the slope with ropes. If drivers tried to drive down the pass, they could lose control down the steep path.

Susan Shelby Magoffin, whose husband was a trader, kept a diary of her 1846 trip. At Raton Pass she wrote, "It takes a dozen men to steady a wagon with all its wheels locked — and for one who is some distance off to hear the crash it makes over the stones is truly alarming." For many, this was the most dangerous part of the journey.

The Mountain Toll

"Uncle Dick" Wootton was a famous sheep herder who purchased part of the Raton Pass in 1865. He sold a huge herd of sheep and used the gold he was paid to buy and blast the steep Raton Pass. The road became smoother and safer. He turned Raton Pass into a toll road. Wootton charged everyone except American Indians to travel his road. Later, this was the road the Santa Fe Railroad used.

Some parts of the pass were so narrow only one wagon could fit across it.

The Mountain Branch and the Cimarron Cutoff came together again in New Mexico, about 75 miles (120 km) south of Raton. The U.S. Army built Fort Union there in 1851. From here, wagons headed south through the New Mexico towns of Las Vegas and Pecos and into Santa Fe.

The trail ended in the Plaza of Santa Fe in front of the 200-year-old Palace of the Governors. All traders had to stop in the plaza so that officials could check and tax their goods. Only then were they free to sell what they had brought.

The local people were eager to buy from traders. They wanted glass windows and bottles, fabrics for new clothing, and small manufactured items such as kitchen tools.

In 1846 an American flag flew above the palace. Four years later, New Mexico became a U.S. territory.

Many traders bought furs and silver goods in New Mexico to sell back east. Traders brought many mules to Missouri from Santa Fe. But the traders never took as many goods back to Missouri as they had brought into New Mexico on the Santa Fe Trail.

ON THE TRAIL

An important book about life on the trail titled *Commerce of the Prairie* was published in 1844. Author Josiah Gregg, the son of a Missouri **wheelwright**, was sent west for his health in 1831. His book became a pioneer's guide of what to expect on the trail. Gregg also wisely predicted that if Americans continued to kill bison for fun, the animal would eventually die out. Thanks to protection efforts, bison have come back from almost being **extinct**.

Gregg traveled the Santa Fe Trail as a passenger, but most people who traveled the Santa Fe Trail were carrying goods by freight. Unlike the Oregon Trail, which brought travelers to the West, the Santa Fe Trail was mainly a freight highway. Freight wagons were larger than their Oregan Trail counterparts, sometimes carrying more than 6,000 pounds (2,725 kg). The wagons of the Oregon Trail carried about 2,000 pounds (900 kg). Teams of eight oxen or eight mules pulled the freight wagons. The men who drove these wagons were called **bullwhackers** or **mule skinners**.

Settlers over-hunted bison for food and sport.

American Bison

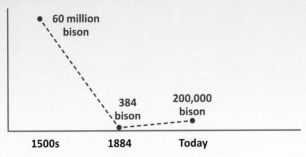

60 million	60 million bison	
	384 bison	200,000 bison
1500s	1884	Today

American bison numbers were estimated to have been 60 million during the 1500s. But during westward expansion, bison numbers fell dangerously low, and they almost became extinct. Now, bison numbers are getting better thanks to national parks and preserves.

DID YOU KNOW?
In the 1840s, a pair of matching mules cost about $400 while a pair of oxen could be bought for $20. Oxen were usually preferred over mules. However, mules could turn to see their hind legs, which provided better balance for mountain passes.

wheelwright—someone who makes and repairs wheels and wheeled vehicles

extinct—no longer living; an extinct animal is one that has died out

bullwhacker—a person who drives a wagon with oxen

mule skinner—a person who drives a wagon with mules

When the terrain made it impossible for the wagons to hold additional weight, women and children walked while the men drove.

Wagons usually traveled in several lines when they could. Then, if they needed protection, they could quickly move into a square with the animals inside. Travelers faced danger from prairie fires, rattlesnakes, and unexpected storms.

Women also made the trip. They usually traveled with their husbands going west to set up businesses. The first known European family to travel the Santa Fe Trail was William and Mary Donoho and their 9-month-old daughter Mary Anne. The Donohos went into the hotel business in Santa Fe before later returning to Missouri.

Marian Russell became another female pioneer of the Santa Fe Trail. She was only 7 years old her first time on the trail in 1852. She made the trip with her mother and brother. She fell in love with the trail and traveled it many times over the years. She later married one of Christopher Carson's soldiers.

Land of Enchantment

Marian Russell married Lieutenant Richard Russell. The couple eventually moved to Stonewall Valley in Colorado to ranch. When Marian was in her 80s, her daughter-in-law wrote down Marian's memories of being on the trail. This became Marian's autobiography, *Land of Enchantment*. Marian died in 1936 at the age of 91. The book was published in 1954, again in 1981, and has been reprinted multiple times.

The Santa Fe Trail had become the lifeblood of the Southwest. By 1860, about 3,000 wagons traveled the trail every year. It took 28,000 oxen and 9,000 men to supply the needs of the people at both ends of the trail and along the way.

This was not lost on the **Confederate States of America**, formed by the southern states during the Civil War (1861–1865). Confederate troops captured Fort Fillmore, near modern-day Las Cruces, New Mexico. With Fort Fillmore captured, Confederates took New Mexico and Arizona in August 1861. Union soldiers retreated to Fort Union, near where the Mountain Branch and the Cimarron Cutoff joined.

The two sides met again at La Glorieta Pass, near Santa Fe, in March 1862. Union troops destroyed all Confederate supplies, and the southerners were driven back into Texas. The Battle of La Glorieta Pass ended the Confederacy's only chance to win the Southwest.

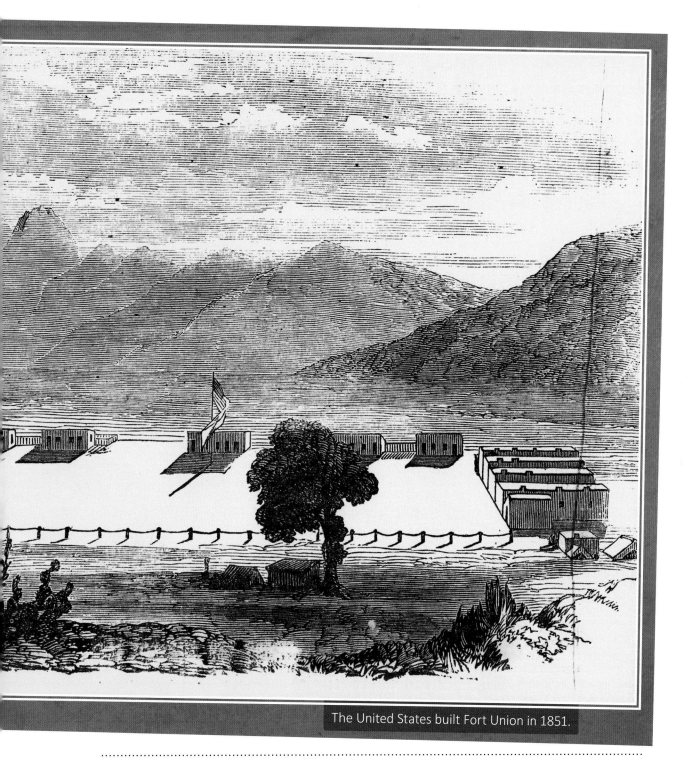

The United States built Fort Union in 1851.

Confederate States of America—the southern states that left the Union and fought against the northern states in the Civil War; also called the Confederacy

THE END OF THE TRAIL

As the Civil War was being fought, noisy **steam engines** were already being heard along part of the Santa Fe Trail. The Atchison, Topeka, and Santa Fe railroads — now the Santa Fe Railroad — were all being built from Kansas to the Southwest. When tracks reached Santa Fe in 1880, the days of the wagon trail were over.

Highways replaced much of the Santa Fe Trail in the 1930s. Marian Russell, in her 90s, recalled, "The old trail over mountains, through forests, felt the sting of the cold . . . the heat, the drench of rains, and the fury of the winds in an old covered wagon." She thought, "My life as I look back seems to have been lived best in those days on the trail."

steam engine—an engine that gets power by heating water to make steam

DID YOU KNOW?
On today's highways, the Santa Fe Trail — from Independence to Santa Fe — covers less than 800 miles (1287 km) and only takes about 12 hours to drive. By wagon, it would take the traders more than eight weeks for the same trip. By plane, the trip is less than four hours.

Pioneers traveled the Santa Fe Trail for almost 60 years before the railroad made it unnecessary.

GLOSSARY

adobe (uh-DOH-bee)—a brick building material made of clay mixed with straw and dried in the sun

apprentice (uh-PREN-tiss)—someone who learns a trade by working with a skilled person

bullwhacker (buhl-WAK-uhr)—a person who drives a wagon with oxen

caravan (KAYR-uh-van)—a group of wagons traveling together

colonist (KAH-luh-nist)—a person who settles in a new territory that is governed by his or her home country

Confederate States of America (kuhn-FE-der-uht STAYTS uhv uh-MER-uh-kuh)—southern states that left the Union and fought against the northern states in the Civil War; also called the Confederacy

culture (KUHL-ture)—a people's way of life, ideas, art, customs, and traditions

extinct (ik-STINGKT)—no longer living; an extinct animal is one that has died out

legend (LEJ-uhnd)—a story passed down through the years that may not be completely true

missionary (MISH-uh-ner-ee)—a person who does religious or charitable work in a territory or foreign country

mule skinner (MYOOL SKIN-uhr)—a person who drives a wagon with mules

reservation (rez-er-VAY-shuhn)—an area of land set aside by the U.S. government for American Indians

steam engine (STEEM EN-juhn)—an engine that gets power by heating water to make steam

wheelwright (weel-RITE)—someone who makes and repairs wheels and wheeled vehicles

CRITICAL THINKING QUESTIONS

1. Why did the Santa Fe Trail become such a popular trade route?

2. Why was Franklin, Missouri, and later Independence, Missouri, the trailhead?

3. If you were on the Santa Fe Trail, which path would you take and why?

READ MORE

Glass, Andrew. *A Right Fine Life: Kit Carson on the Santa Fe Trail.* Concord, Mass.: StarWalk Kids Media, 2014.

Kamma, Anne. *If You Were a Pioneer on the Prairie.* If You. New York: Scholastic Inc., 2014.

Winters, Kay. *Voices from the Oregon Trail.* New York: Dial Books, 2014.

INTERNET SITES

Use Facthound to find Internet sites related to this book.

Visit *www.facthound.com*

Just type in 9781515771159 and go!

Check out projects, games and lots more at
www.capstonekids.com

INDEX